RELEASING HEAVEN'S POWER

EMBRACING THE GIFTS OF THE SPIRIT

TOM CORNELL

RELEASING HEAVEN'S POWER

Embracing the Gifts of the Spirit

TOM CORNELL

SOZO PUBLISHING

Paperback ISBN: 978-1-969882-00-5

Contents

Introduction

In the life of the Church, the gifts of the Holy Spirit are not just tools for personal enrichment; they are the very instruments of God's divine power, given to transform lives and advance His Kingdom. These gifts—outlined in 1 Corinthians 12—are living, active expressions of God's supernatural presence, meant to be embraced by every believer, not as relics of the past, but as gifts to be sought after, activated, and practiced in the present day.

Yet despite their biblical foundation, many believers struggle with misunderstanding, fear, or doubt when it comes to spiritual gifts. This hesitation often prevents them from stepping fully into the transformative power that God has made available. Some worry about misusing or misunderstanding these gifts, while others feel unworthy or ill-equipped to operate in them. But the truth is clear: the gifts of the Holy Spirit are for all believers, not just a select few. They are given by God, not based on our own merit but because of His love and desire to empower us to build up the body of Christ and advance His mission on earth.

This book is a call to action—a call to embrace the fullness of what God has provided through His gifts of the Spirit. The purpose of this journey is not merely to inform but to activate. It is not enough to understand these gifts; we must walk in them, exercise them, and see them released into our lives and communities. Spiritual gifts are meant to serve the body of Christ, to unite believers in love, and to promote spiritual health and growth. They are not for personal glory or self-enrichment, but for the edification of the Church and the expansion of God's Kingdom.

The exercise of these gifts requires more than intellectual knowledge—it demands faith and courage. As we step out in trust and boldness, we allow God to move through us in powerful ways, making His presence known in our lives and in the world. Too many believers are missing out on the fullness of God's power because they hold back in fear or uncertainty. But when we walk by faith, we become conduits of God's supernatural power, bringing heaven to earth in every situation we face

This book will guide you in understanding each of the nine gifts of the Spirit: what they are, how to recognize them, and most importantly, how to operate in them with boldness and love. As you embrace these gifts, you will not only experience personal transformation but also become an active participant in God's grand mission on earth. It is time for the Church to rediscover the power and purpose of the gifts of the Holy Spirit. It is time to release Heaven's power in the Church today.

The Kingdom of God is advancing, and the gifts of the Holy Spirit are essential for that advancement. It is time for you, as a believer, to step forward with confidence and embrace the gifts God has freely given to you. Together, as the body of Christ, we can walk in the fullness of God's power and fulfill our mission to make His presence known in a world in desperate need of transformation.

Understanding Spiritual Gifts
EMPOWERED FOR SERVICE

*S*piritual gifts are not optional accessories in the life of a believer—they are essential. They are divine tools given by the Holy Spirit to empower believers to fulfill God's mission on Earth. Far from being mere charismatic manifestations, these gifts are God's chosen means to build up the body of Christ, advance His Kingdom, and extend His glory throughout the world. Every believer has access to all nine spiritual gifts. While some may experience stronger manifestations in certain areas, the Holy Spirit can activate any of these gifts in the life of a believer as needed, whether in a church service or out in the marketplace.

Understanding the biblical foundation of spiritual gifts is key to walking in their fullness. In his writings, the Apostle Paul provides clarity on the nature, purpose, and operation of spiritual gifts, especially in 1 Corinthians 12, Romans 12, and Ephesians 4. These passages highlight that spiritual gifts are not earned through effort or spiritual achievement, but are freely given by God's grace. They are manifestations of God's love, given to His children for the common good and to fulfill the Great Commission.

One of the most beautiful aspects of spiritual gifts is their diversity. The Holy Spirit distributes these gifts as He wills, ensuring that every believer has access to the full range of spiritual gifts. While some individuals may feel more attuned to certain gifts, the Holy Spirit is free to activate any of them in each believer as needed. This intentional diversity serves to complement one another, creating a unified body where each part is indispensable. Spiritual gifts are not about personal advancement; they are tools for God's larger purpose —advancing His Kingdom on Earth. The beauty of this diversity is that it fosters mutual growth, support, and accountability, helping the Church move forward in its mission.

A common misconception about spiritual gifts is that they are reserved only for a select few—those in leadership positions or spiritually mature believers. However, Scripture makes it clear that every believer has access to these gifts. Spiritual gifts are not for the elite; they are for all who follow Christ. Whether you are a new believer or a seasoned disciple, the Holy Spirit has equipped you with the ability to flow in all the gifts. This means no one is excluded or disqualified from exercising their spiritual gifts. Every believer has a unique role to play in God's plan, and each is essential for the growth and health of the Church.

The process of identifying and developing the spiritual gifts is essential to fulfilling your calling in Christ. It begins with prayer, seeking God's guidance, and immersing yourself in Scripture. Sometimes, understanding the gifts in your life will be aided by the insights of mature believers who can confirm what the Holy Spirit is revealing to you. But at the core of this process is humility. Spiritual gifts are not for self-glorification; they are meant to serve others. As you grow in the gifts, remember that they are a reflection of God's grace and His desire to work through you for His glory and the good of others.

However, there is one principle that must guide the exercise of all spiritual gifts: love. Without love, spiritual gifts become empty exercises of power. As Paul writes in 1 Corinthians 13, even the most extraordinary gifts are meaningless without love. Love is the foundation that ensures spiritual gifts are used with pure motives. When spiritual gifts are exercised in love, they become powerful tools for edification, encouragement, correction, and healing within the body of Christ. Love transforms the exercise of spiritual gifts from mere displays of power to genuine expressions of God's heart.

The ultimate goal of spiritual gifts is to build up the Church and advance God's Kingdom. Love ensures that this goal is achieved. As believers, we must constantly evaluate our use of spiritual gifts, asking ourselves if we are exercising them with love and for the good of others. This self-reflection helps us mature and ensures that the gifts are not used for personal gain, but to fulfill God's purposes. When we operate in the gifts with love, we are participating in the divine work of advancing God's Kingdom and bringing glory to His name.

In conclusion, spiritual gifts are essential for believers to fulfill their divine calling and serve God's Kingdom. The diversity of these gifts reflects the wisdom of the Holy Spirit, and their purpose is to build up the body of Christ, advance God's work, and bring glory to His name. It is critical that every believer understands, embraces, and develops the gifts of the spirit in humility and love. As we do, we allow the Holy Spirit to work powerfully through us, fulfilling the mission of the Church and impacting the world with the love and power of God.

Reflection Questions:

1. In what areas of your life have you seen the Holy Spirit activate spiritual gifts in you? Are there gifts you feel more drawn to, and how have they been used to serve others?
2. How can you ensure that the gifts you operate in are motivated by love rather than self-promotion? What steps can you take to evaluate your motives when exercising spiritual gifts?

Challenge:

THIS WEEK, pray for the Holy Spirit to reveal the spiritual gifts He has already placed within you. Ask Him to highlight areas where you can step out in faith to use those gifts for the building up of the body of Christ and to serve others—whether in your church, workplace, or community. Take one intentional step to exercise one of your spiritual gifts with love and humility, looking for opportunities to bless those around you.

Understanding How the Holy Spirit Moves
PARTNERING WITH DIVINE GUIDANCE

*T*he Holy Spirit is not just a force or an abstract concept, but a divine person actively at work in the world today. Understanding how He moves is essential for believers who desire to effectively operate in spiritual gifts. Spiritual gifts are expressions of the Holy Spirit's presence and power, and as such, they are closely linked to His movements. In order to operate in these gifts, believers must first recognize and partner with the Holy Spirit's work.

The Holy Spirit operates in diverse ways, and these movements are often tailored to the specific needs of individuals and communities. Looking at Scripture, we can see that His work adapts to the context of each generation. For example, in the Old Testament, the Spirit came upon prophets like Elijah and Elisha, empowering them for specific tasks. In the New Testament, the Holy Spirit rested upon Jesus at His baptism and later filled the disciples at Pentecost. These examples demonstrate that the Holy Spirit's work is both dynamic and intentional, always aligning with God's overarching purpose of glorifying Himself.

One of the key aspects of partnering with the Holy Spirit is cultivating sensitivity to His presence. To be sensitive to the Holy Spirit, believers must develop an intimate relationship with Him. This is not something that can be forced through rules or formulas but is a result of an ongoing, deepening connection with God. Through practices such as prayer, worship, and meditation on the Word of God, believers can become more attuned to the subtle ways the Holy Spirit moves and speaks, allowing them to recognize His promptings in their daily lives.

Obedience is another critical factor in partnering with the Holy Spirit. When believers respond promptly to His leading, they make room for the Holy Spirit to work powerfully through them. Delayed or hesitant responses can stifle the flow of spiritual gifts and hinder the work God wants to do through us. Throughout Scripture, we see examples of individuals who acted quickly in response to the Spirit's prompting, leading to powerful manifestations of His power and presence. Our obedience to the Holy Spirit's guidance opens the door for greater expressions of His gifts and purposes in the world.

While personal sensitivity to the Holy Spirit is important, the corporate dimension of His movement is equally significant. The Holy Spirit often moves in gatherings of believers, creating an atmosphere where spiritual gifts can be released for the benefit of all. As believers come together in faith and unity, they create an environment where the Holy Spirit can move freely and powerfully. Leaders play a key role in fostering this atmosphere by encouraging faith, expectation, and unity within the body of Christ. When the church gathers with a collective heart to welcome the Holy Spirit, spiritual gifts are more readily manifested and shared among the congregation.

It is essential to avoid trying to control or manipulate the Holy Spirit's work. The Holy Spirit is not to be boxed into formulas or rigid methods. Rather, believers are called to surrender and trust the Spirit's guidance moment by moment. This posture of surrender fosters a deeper trust in the Holy Spirit's wisdom and timing, ensuring that spiritual gifts are exercised authentically and in alignment with God's will. Trusting the Spirit allows believers to step into the flow of His work without trying to orchestrate it ourselves.

A surrendered heart leads to a deeper understanding of how the Holy Spirit moves, positioning believers to be effective vessels for His work. By cultivating sensitivity, practicing obedience, and embracing surrender, believers can more fully partner with the Holy Spirit in releasing His gifts and fulfilling God's purposes on Earth. In this way, they become conduits of His power, bringing transformation to their communities and advancing the Kingdom of God.

In conclusion, understanding the dynamics of how the Holy Spirit moves is essential for believers who wish to operate in spiritual gifts. The Holy Spirit is not just a passive force but a living, active presence that desires to work through His people. As we cultivate sensitivity, obedience, and surrender, we position ourselves to cooperate with His work and release His gifts for the benefit of the body of Christ and the advancement of His Kingdom. By embracing the Holy Spirit's leading, we step into the flow of divine power, fulfilling our calling to be vessels of God's glory.

Reflection Questions:

1. How would you describe your current level of sensitivity to the Holy Spirit's presence? What practices or habits could you develop to cultivate a deeper relationship with Him?
2. Reflect on a time when you felt the Holy Spirit prompting you to act. How did you respond, and what was the outcome? What can you learn from this experience to improve your obedience in the future?

Challenge:

THIS WEEK, take time to intentionally seek the Holy Spirit's guidance in both your daily activities and your spiritual life. Focus on cultivating sensitivity through prayer and listening, and be open to any promptings He may give. When you sense His leading, respond with prompt obedience, trusting that He will guide you in fulfilling God's purposes.

3

Exercising Spiritual Gifts
DEVELOPING RESPONSIBILITY AND MATURITY

*S*piritual gifts are powerful tools given by the Holy Spirit to build up the body of Christ. However, it is crucial to understand that these gifts are not for personal glory but are meant to edify and serve others. When exercising spiritual gifts, one must approach them with humility and a servant's heart. Spiritual gifts are not tools for self-promotion; they are divine resources entrusted to us for the advancement of God's Kingdom and the benefit of the church.

The development of spiritual gifts is similar to the cultivation of natural talents. While spiritual gifts are given by grace, they require intentional effort and practice to grow. Just as a person refines their skills through repeated effort, one must nurture the gifts by using them regularly and learning from both their successes and their failures. Growth in spiritual gifts happens through stepping out in faith, persevering through challenges, and continually relying on the Holy Spirit for guidance and empowerment.

A key aspect of exercising spiritual gifts responsibly is accountability. It is essential to operate under spiritual covering and within the context of a healthy church community. Trusted leaders and mentors provide valuable support and guidance as individuals learn to exercise the gifts. This accountability prevents misuse and ensures that gifts are exercised in a way that honors God and benefits others. Operating in community helps keep the gifts in check, ensuring they are used responsibly and in alignment with God's purposes.

To develop spiritual gifts, one should engage in regular prayer, study of Scripture, and seek opportunities to serve others. By immersing oneself in these practices, they create spaces where they can practice and grow in the gifts. Whether through small groups, prayer meetings, or everyday interactions, one should be intentional about stepping out in faith and exercising the gifts. As they do, they will sharpen their ability to discern the Holy Spirit's leading, increase their confidence, and grow in their effectiveness in ministry.

While spiritual gifts demonstrate the power of God, it is one's character that sustains and supports their use. It is important to develop a Christlike character alongside the use of spiritual gifts. If a person's character does not grow in tandem with the gifts, there is a risk that pride, arrogance, or immaturity could undermine their effectiveness. Gifts, when exercised with love and integrity, become powerful instruments in building up the church. Developing a Christlike character ensures that gifts are used in the right way, with the right motives, and for the glory of God.

Exercising spiritual gifts also involves overcoming challenges, such as fear, doubt, and making mistakes. Mistakes are a natural part of the learning process, and one should not be discouraged when they occur. Instead of letting failures hinder progress, one should remain teachable and seek feedback from trusted mentors. This helps cultivate a healthy, growth-oriented mindset that is essential for personal development and effectiveness in using spiritual gifts.

As one steps out in faith, they should balance boldness with wisdom. Boldness is necessary to exercise spiritual gifts, but wisdom ensures that they are used appropriately and responsibly. This balance is critical for long-term growth and maturity in the gifts. By cultivating diligence, humility, and accountability, one can mature into an effective vessel through whom the Holy Spirit works. As they grow in wisdom and character, the gifts will become a more powerful tools for ministry and for advancing the Kingdom of God.

In conclusion, exercising spiritual gifts requires a combination of spiritual principles and practical application. One must approach the gifts with a sense of responsibility, nurturing them with diligence, humility, and accountability. By developing character alongside gifts, and remaining teachable and responsive to feedback, they position themselves to be effective ministers. Through this balanced approach, one can grow into a mature vessel through whom the Holy Spirit works, building up the church and fulfilling God's purposes in the world.

Reflection Questions:

1. How can you intentionally nurture and develop the spiritual gifts to serve others, and what practical steps can you take this week to grow in using them?
2. In what ways can you ensure that your character aligns with the spiritual gifts you have been entrusted with, and how can you avoid pride or immaturity as you exercise them?

Challenge:

THIS WEEK, take one step of faith to exercise the gifts in service to others—whether it's through a prayer for healing, or a word of encouragement. Be intentional about seeking feedback from a mentor or trusted leader to ensure that you are using the gifts in a way that honors God and builds up the body of Christ.

4

The Gift of Discerning of Spirits
NAVIGATING THE SPIRITUAL REALM

*T*he gift of discerning of spirits is a unique and vital spiritual ability that allows believers to perceive and distinguish between various spiritual influences. This gift enables individuals to discern whether a spirit is divine, human, or demonic. It is essential for maintaining spiritual clarity, protection, and integrity in both personal lives and within the broader church community. By operating in this gift, believers can safeguard themselves from spiritual deception and navigate the complexities of the spiritual realm with confidence.

At the heart of discerning of spirits is the ability to recognize the true nature of spiritual forces at work. In 1 Corinthians 12:10, the Apostle Paul lists this gift among the manifestations of the Holy Spirit. Throughout Scripture, we see clear examples of individuals using this gift to discern spiritual realities. Jesus demonstrated this ability when He perceived the thoughts and intentions of people's hearts (John 2:24-25), and the Apostle Paul displayed it when he recognized a spirit of divination in a young slave girl (Acts 16:16-18).

These biblical accounts show that discerning of spirits is not only a practical gift but one that serves to bring greater understanding and clarity in a world full of spiritual confusion.

The primary purpose of this gift is to protect believers from deception and harm. In today's world, where false teachings and counterfeit spiritual movements are prevalent, the gift of discerning spirits becomes crucial. By distinguishing between true and false spiritual influences, believers can embrace what is good and reject what is harmful. This discernment helps guard against being led astray by deceptive doctrines or counterfeit spiritual experiences. A foundation rooted in Scripture and a sensitivity to the Holy Spirit are key to cultivating this gift and sharpening one's ability to discern effectively.

Discerning of spirits is not only about detecting harmful influences but also about understanding the true motives of others. This relational aspect of the gift allows believers to see beyond outward appearances and understand what is happening in the spiritual realm. However, it is important to approach this gift with humility and love. The goal is not to judge or control others but to bring clarity and understanding, offering protection and healing where needed. The exercise of this gift should always be done with a heart for restoration, not condemnation, ensuring that others are built up in their faith.

In addition to its protective role, discerning of spirits is also essential for engaging in spiritual warfare. Believers operating in this gift are often able to detect the presence of demonic forces or strategies that may be hindering God's work. With this discernment, believers can pray more effectively, binding spirits and proclaiming the authority of God over spiritual opposition. Spiritual warfare requires preparedness and vigilance, and discerning of spirits equips individuals to respond with the right tools, wisdom, and spiritual authority.

The gift of discerning of spirits is not limited to detecting negative influences; it also plays a role in recognizing divine activity. Believers can discern the presence of angels, the Holy Spirit's movement, or other manifestations of God's power. Being sensitive to these moments opens the door for greater spiritual encounters and breakthroughs. Recognizing divine activity can lead to greater empowerment in ministry and a deeper connection to the work that God is doing in the world.

As believers cultivate and exercise this gift, they are called to approach it with a deep sense of humility and dependence on the Holy Spirit. The gift of discerning of spirits should not be used as a tool for personal gain or to elevate one's spiritual status. Instead, it is a gift to be stewarded with responsibility, always aligning with God's purposes. The fruit of this gift is seen in lives transformed by truth, individuals protected from deception, and communities built up in love.

In conclusion, the gift of discerning of spirits equips believers to navigate the spiritual realm with wisdom and discernment. It is a crucial gift for spiritual protection, relational clarity, and effective spiritual warfare. As believers seek to grow in this gift, they must remain humble, rooted in Scripture, and sensitive to the Holy Spirit's leading. Through the proper use of this gift, the body of Christ can experience greater freedom, protection, and advancement of God's Kingdom.

Reflection Questions:

1. How can you cultivate a deeper sensitivity to the Holy Spirit to strengthen your ability to discern spiritual influences in your life and the lives of others?
2. In what areas of your life or ministry could the gift of discerning of spirits be particularly beneficial, and how can you ensure you are using it with humility and a heart for restoration?

Challenge:

THIS WEEK, take time to prayerfully discern the spiritual atmosphere in your environment—whether at work, in relationships, or within the church. Ask the Holy Spirit to reveal any false influences or divine movements, and respond in faith through prayer or intercession. Make sure to approach this process with humility, seeking not to judge, but to bring clarity, protection, and restoration where needed.

5

The Gift of the Word of Wisdom
DIVINE INSIGHT FOR DECISION MAKING

The word of wisdom is a powerful spiritual gift that provides divine insight and guidance, enabling believers to navigate complex situations in alignment with God's will. This gift goes beyond natural wisdom or intellect, offering a supernatural impartation from the Holy Spirit that brings clarity, direction, and practical solutions. It is essential for believers who seek to make decisions that are in harmony with God's purposes, particularly in moments of uncertainty or difficulty.

In Scripture, the word of wisdom is identified as one of the gifts of the Holy Spirit, as noted in 1 Corinthians 12:8. Throughout the Bible, we see key figures who exemplified this gift, such as Joseph, Solomon, and Daniel. For instance, Joseph's ability to interpret Pharaoh's dreams and devise a plan to save Egypt during a time of famine (Genesis 41) is a prime example of the word of wisdom in action. These biblical instances demonstrate that the word of wisdom can be a divinely inspired solution that not only brings clarity but also provides practical steps for navigating life's challenges.

The gift of the word of wisdom often operates in real-life scenarios that require more than human reasoning. It is particularly relevant when believers face situations that are too complex or difficult to solve with natural understanding. The word of wisdom may come in various forms, including prophetic impressions, visions, dreams, or even a sudden knowing within one's spirit. The Holy Spirit can reveal divine wisdom in moments of great need, and it is crucial for believers to remain sensitive to the Spirit's leading in order to recognize and respond to this gift.

It is important to distinguish the word of wisdom from other spiritual gifts, especially the word of knowledge. While the word of knowledge involves receiving specific factual information supernaturally, the word of wisdom provides the guidance on how to apply that knowledge in a way that aligns with God's will. These two gifts often work together—knowledge provides the revelation, and wisdom offers the next steps. The word of wisdom takes the insight gained from the word of knowledge and translates it into a practical, actionable plan that honors God's purposes.

Exercising the word of wisdom requires faith and humility. Since the gift involves divine insight, it demands trust in God's ability to guide and provide the answers needed. Believers must be cautious not to approach this gift with arrogance or presumption. The word of wisdom is meant to serve others and glorify God, not to elevate one's own status. In critical situations, it is essential to seek confirmation of the wisdom received, whether through

Scripture, prayer, or trusted spiritual leaders, to ensure that the guidance is truly from God.

To cultivate the gift of the word of wisdom, believers must spend time in prayer, study the Word of God, and develop a habit of listening to the Holy Spirit in everyday life. The gift is most effective when believers live in close relationship with God, remaining obedient to His voice. By seeking God's wisdom in both small and large decisions, believers can grow in their ability to discern and apply divine insight, allowing them to navigate life's challenges with confidence and clarity.

The word of wisdom is not just for personal decision making but is also essential in corporate settings, where the body of Christ may need guidance on how to move forward in fulfilling God's purposes. The gift enables leaders and believers alike to make decisions that bring peace, clarity, and direction to complex situations. In both personal and communal contexts, the word of wisdom can bring understanding and solutions that are aligned with God's will and plan.

In conclusion, the word of wisdom is a vital spiritual gift that equips believers to make sound decisions and navigate life's complexities with divine insight. It is a tool that brings clarity and direction, helping believers align their choices with God's purposes. By relying on the Holy Spirit and staying rooted in God's Word, believers can become vessels through whom divine wisdom flows, bringing peace and clarity in challenging situations. The word of wisdom is an invaluable gift that believers should seek and cultivate to fulfill God's call on their lives and ministries.

Reflection Questions:

1. In what areas of your life do you feel a need for divine insight or guidance, and how can you actively seek the gift of the word of wisdom to navigate these situations?

2. How can you distinguish between your own understanding and the Holy Spirit's guidance when seeking wisdom for decision-making, and what practical steps can you take to stay sensitive to His leading?

Challenge:

THIS WEEK, find a challenging situation in your personal or ministry life where you need direction. Commit to praying and asking the Holy Spirit for the word of wisdom, trusting Him to provide clear guidance. As you wait for insight, be open to receiving it through Scripture, a trusted mentor, or a moment of quiet reflection. After receiving guidance, take practical steps in faith and humility, and seek confirmation through prayer or further counsel to ensure the wisdom is aligned with God's will.

The Gift of the Word of Knowledge
DIVINE REVELATION FOR TRANSFORMATION

*T*he word of knowledge is a supernatural gift that provides specific revelation about a person, situation, or circumstance. It is a divine impartation of knowledge given by the Holy Spirit, often at moments when human understanding or reasoning falls short. Unlike natural knowledge, which is acquired through education and experience, the word of knowledge reveals hidden truths or details that can only come from God. This gift demonstrates God's intimate care for His people, offering them insights that guide, encourage, and protect them in various situations.

In the Bible, the word of knowledge is identified as one of the gifts of the Holy Spirit in 1 Corinthians 12:8. The Apostle Paul mentions it alongside other gifts that empower believers to operate supernaturally. One of the most powerful examples of the word of knowledge in action is found in the life of Jesus. In John 4:16-19, Jesus reveals to the Samaritan woman at the well details of her life—information that He could not have known through natural means. This encounter not only demonstrates divine knowledge but also leads to her transformation and the salvation of many in her community. The word of knowledge can be a powerful tool in revealing God's heart and bringing people closer to Him.

The gift of the word of knowledge can come in various forms. Some believers may receive it as an inner knowing, while others may experience it through dreams, visions, or impressions. Each person may encounter the gift differently, as the Holy Spirit tailors His communication to the individual. However, the key to recognizing when a word of knowledge is being given is cultivating sensitivity to the Holy Spirit's voice. By engaging in regular prayer, worship, and quiet reflection, believers can train themselves to hear and discern God's voice, which is crucial in recognizing moments when this gift is operating.

The purpose of the word of knowledge is not to showcase one's abilities or to control others, but to bring healing, encouragement, and direction. It is a manifestation of God's love for His people, showing them that He sees their needs and cares deeply about their lives. When exercised properly, the word of knowledge can open doors for ministry, bringing comfort to the brokenhearted, guidance to the confused, and hope to those in despair. It is a tool that can help point people toward God's will and plan for their lives, offering clarity in times of uncertainty.

In exercising the word of knowledge, it is essential for believers to use the gift with humility and love. The focus should always remain on glorifying God, not drawing attention to the one delivering the word. Believers should also be cautious when sharing the word, especially if it involves personal or sensitive information. Seeking confirmation from the Holy Spirit, Scripture, and trusted spiritual leaders ensures that the word is accurate and aligned with God's will. This step helps avoid misinterpretation or misuse of the gift, ensuring that it serves its intended purpose.

Another important consideration when using the word of knowledge is presenting it in a way that fosters faith, hope, and healing. The information received through this gift should be shared in a manner that encourages the recipient, rather than causing them to feel judged or condemned. The goal is to create a safe environment where individuals can receive the revelation in a positive and transformative way. By sharing the word with grace and sensitivity, believers can minister effectively, ensuring that the recipient experiences God's love and care through the gift.

The word of knowledge often works in tandem with other spiritual gifts, such as prophecy and healing. For instance, receiving specific knowledge about a person's condition or need can open the door for prayer and healing. The word of knowledge may also serve as a confirmation of God's plan, paving the way for prophetic words or actions that bring further clarity and direction. When combined, these gifts can lead to powerful breakthroughs in individuals' lives, ministries, and communities.

In conclusion, the word of knowledge is a vital spiritual gift that allows believers to receive divine insight and understanding into people, situations, and circumstances. It operates as a tool for God's guidance, encouragement, and intervention, revealing His heart for His people. To effectively exercise this gift, believers must cultivate a close relationship with the Holy Spirit, ensuring that they are sensitive to His voice and humble in their approach. When used with love and humility, the word of knowledge can bring healing, hope, and transformation to those in need, advancing God's Kingdom on Earth.

Reflection Questions:

1. How have you experienced the gift of the word of knowledge in your own life or in the lives of others? How did it impact you or those involved?

2. What steps can you take to cultivate a deeper sensitivity to the Holy Spirit's voice so you can recognize when the word of knowledge is being imparted to you?

Challenge:

THIS WEEK, ask the Holy Spirit to reveal a specific word of knowledge to you for someone in your life. Spend time in prayer and quiet reflection, seeking His guidance. When you receive the word, share it with the individual in love and humility, ensuring it brings comfort, direction, or healing. Afterward, reflect on how God used this gift to bring His kingdom to earth and deepen your relationship with Him.

7

The Gift of Faith
TRUSTING GOD FOR THE IMPOSSIBLE

*T*he gift of faith is a supernatural empowerment from the Holy Spirit that enables believers to trust God in extraordinary ways. Unlike the foundational faith that every Christian possesses for salvation, the gift of faith is a specific, divine confidence that empowers believers to act boldly and trust in God's intervention in miraculous situations. This special gift is not about human effort or natural belief, but rather about an unshakable confidence in God's promises and His ability to act in ways that defy human logic and natural limitations.

In 1 Corinthians 12:9, the Apostle Paul lists the gift of faith as one of the nine spiritual gifts, providing a biblical foundation for this supernatural endowment. This gift is not something believers can muster on their own; it is a divine impartation from the Holy Spirit that enables them to trust God in situations where the natural world offers no solutions. Throughout Scripture, we see this gift at work in powerful moments of divine breakthrough. For example, when Elijah called down fire from heaven on Mount Carmel (1 Kings 18) or when Peter walked on water (Matthew 14:28-29), these miraculous events were made possible by the gift of faith—trusting God beyond what human reasoning could comprehend.

The gift of faith operates at critical moments when human effort or reasoning falls short. It often comes in response to the prompting of the Holy Spirit, empowering believers to step into situations that appear impossible by natural standards. This gift is not wishful thinking, nor is it presumption; rather, it is an unwavering confidence in God's ability to act according to His will and timing. It requires a close relationship with God, a readiness to hear His voice, and an alignment with His purposes before stepping out in faith.

The gift of faith can manifest in various contexts, such as healing, deliverance, provision, and protection. In these situations, the believer's confidence in God leads to supernatural outcomes. When believers operate in the gift of faith, they may see divine provision in times of lack, healing in the face of sickness, and protection when danger is near. This gift enables believers to trust God for results that go beyond natural capabilities, leading to lifechanging transformations both for individuals and communities.

To cultivate the gift of faith, believers must immerse themselves in spiritual practices such as reading Scripture, prayer, and worship. These practices strengthen the believer's relationship with God and create an environment in which faith can grow.

Additionally, being part of a community that operates in faith is essential. The collective faith of a united body can inspire and activate the gift of faith within individuals. It is also crucial to guard against fear and doubt, as these can block the flow of faith and hinder the believer from stepping out in trust.

Humility is an essential aspect of exercising the gift of faith. The believer must recognize that this gift comes solely from the Holy Spirit and must always be used for God's glory, not for personal gain or self-promotion. Arrogance or self-reliance can distort the purpose of the gift, and so the believer must remain humble, continually seeking God's direction and guidance. This humility ensures that the gift of faith is used in alignment with God's will and for the benefit of others, not for personal agendas.

When believers step out in the gift of faith, they are invited to enter into the realm of the miraculous. Through personal testimonies and the experiences of others, we see how the gift of faith leads to extraordinary outcomes. The believer is called to cultivate a deeper relationship with God, to listen attentively for His voice, and to step forward in bold confidence when prompted by the Holy Spirit. In doing so, they become vessels through which God's miraculous power flows, bringing healing, hope, and transformation to a hurting world.

The gift of faith empowers believers not only to trust God for personal needs but also to become conduits of His miraculous power to others. It requires a deep trust in God's ability to perform the impossible, both for personal breakthrough and for the well-being of those around them. The believer who operates in the gift of faith can witness God's glory revealed through seemingly impossible circumstances, leading to powerful transformations for individuals, communities, and nations.

In conclusion, the gift of faith is a powerful and supernatural gift that enables believers to trust God for miraculous results. It requires a deep relationship with God, a humble heart, and the willingness to step out in faith when prompted by the Holy Spirit. As believers activate and cultivate this gift, they become conduits of God's miraculous power, witnessing the impossible become possible, all for His glory. The gift of faith is an invitation to experience God's power and to participate in the divine unfolding of His purposes in the world.

Reflection Questions:

1. How can I discern when the Holy Spirit is prompting me to step out in the gift of faith, especially in situations where human reasoning or natural solutions seem impossible?
2. In what areas of my life do I need to grow in trust and confidence in God's promises, and how can I actively cultivate a deeper relationship with Him to strengthen my faith?

Challenge:

THIS WEEK, take time to seek God in prayer and ask Him for the gift of faith in a specific area of your life. Whether it's for provision, healing, or a breakthrough in a difficult situation, step out in boldness and trust that God can intervene in miraculous ways. Stay attuned to His voice, and allow the Holy Spirit to guide you in using this gift for His glory, not for personal gain. Keep a journal of any steps you take in faith, and record the results as a testimony of God's power at work in your life.

8

Becoming Conduits of Divine Healing
PARTNERING WITH THE HOLY SPIRIT

*T*he gifts of healings are a vital part of the believer's spiritual toolkit, enabling them to be conduits of God's healing power in the world. These gifts, as described in 1 Corinthians 12:9, are supernatural manifestations of the Holy Spirit, allowing believers to bring physical, emotional, and spiritual healing to others. Healing is a core aspect of God's kingdom, and believers are called to partner with the Holy Spirit in releasing His healing touch to restore people in every area of life.

While all believers have access to healing through prayer and faith, the gifts of healings are a distinct manifestation of God's power, operating in specific circumstances to bring miraculous restoration. These gifts transcend natural means and can manifest in a variety of ways, such as through the laying on of hands, words of knowledge, or even during worship or prayer. The supernatural nature of these gifts highlights the reality that God can work beyond the limitations of human understanding and ability.

A key element of the gifts of healings is their diversity. Healing is not confined to physical ailments alone; it can address emotional, mental, and spiritual needs as well. The Holy Spirit tailors the manifestation of healing to the unique needs of each individual, whether it involves physical healing, inner healing from past trauma, emotional restoration, or deliverance from spiritual oppression. God's healing power is comprehensive, restoring wholeness in all areas of life.

The ultimate purpose of the gifts of healings is not merely to alleviate suffering but to point to the glory of God. Healing serves as a sign of God's power and love, drawing people to Christ and bringing them into a deeper relationship with Him. Believers must approach healing with a sense of reverence, recognizing that they are partnering with the Holy Spirit in God's mission to bring wholeness to a broken world. Through healing, God's goodness and love are made evident to those in need, leading them to a place of transformation.

Faith is a crucial component in the healing process. While the gifts of healings are supernatural, they often require a step of faith from the believer in order to release God's power. Believers must walk in faith, trusting that God will act according to His will. It is important to approach the ministry of healing with expectancy, believing that God will work miracles as He chooses. Additionally, believers are encouraged to persevere in prayer and ministry, even when immediate results are not seen. Sometimes, the breakthrough takes time, but through continued faith and persistence, healing can be manifested.

Sensitivity to the Holy Spirit is vital when operating in the gifts of healings. Believers must listen to God's voice, discerning His timing and being obedient to His leading. Healing ministry is not about simply offering prayers but about being responsive to how the Holy Spirit directs the believer in each situation. This means being patient and compassionate, recognizing that God's healing process may look different for each person. Some may experience immediate healing, while others may go through a gradual process of restoration.

Believers are also encouraged to minister healing in a way that reflects God's heart for people. Healing is a personal, intimate experience, and each person's journey is unique. It is important to approach each situation with empathy and understanding, trusting that God's healing power is at work in ways that may not always be immediately visible. Healing often involves walking alongside individuals through their process of restoration, offering support, prayer, and encouragement as they experience God's touch in their lives.

The corporate body of believers plays a significant role in the ministry of healing. Healing often happens in the context of a faith-filled community, where believers can come together in unity and agreement. The power of corporate prayer and the atmosphere of faith can activate the gifts of healings, making it easier for God's power to flow freely. A strong community of believers who are sensitive to the Holy Spirit can create an environment where healing becomes a natural expression of God's presence.

In conclusion: The gifts of healings are a powerful demonstration of God's love and power in the world. They are not just for the person receiving healing but for the glory of God and the advancement of His kingdom. As believers, it is essential to cultivate a close relationship with the Holy Spirit, remain sensitive to His guidance, and step out in faith to minister healing to others. Through the gifts of healings, believers can bring restoration and transformation to individuals, communities, and even nations, making God's love known in tangible and miraculous ways.

Healing is not just about the physical restoration of individuals but about bringing people into a deeper encounter with God. When believers operate in the gifts of healings, they become instruments of God's restoration, helping to bring wholeness to a broken world. By embracing these gifts and walking in faith, believers can see God's power released in their lives and in the lives of others, advancing His kingdom and bringing glory to His name.

Reflection Questions:

1. How can you cultivate a deeper sensitivity to the Holy Spirit in your life so that you are more attuned to His guidance when it comes to ministering healing to others?
2. In what ways can you step out in faith to partner with the Holy Spirit in bringing healing —whether physical, emotional, or spiritual—to those around you, even if you don't immediately see the results?

Challenge:

THIS WEEK, take time to pray and ask the Holy Spirit to reveal someone in your life who needs healing. Step out in faith to minister to that person, whether through prayer, encouragement, or simply being present with them. Trust that God will guide you in how to approach the situation, and be open to how He may use you to bring His healing power to them.

9

The Working of Miracles
THE POWER OF DIVINE
INTERVENTION

*I*n the spiritual journey of believers, the gift of the working of miracles stands as one of the most awe-inspiring and transformative expressions of God's power. This extraordinary gift transcends the limits of natural law, offering a demonstration of God's sovereignty and His ability to intervene in human affairs in ways that defy explanation. Miracles are acts of divine power that reveal the might of God, offering a glimpse of His kingdom breaking into the present reality. Through the working of miracles, believers can witness firsthand the supernatural nature of God's love, mercy, and authority.

Miracles have always been an integral part of God's interaction with humanity, seen throughout Scripture as signs of His divine nature and intervention. From the parting of the Red Sea to the resurrection of Jesus Christ, God has used miracles to display His greatness and draw people to Himself. In the New Testament, the apostle Paul speaks of the working of miracles as one of the gifts of the Spirit in 1 Corinthians 12:10. This supernatural ability enables believers to partner with the Holy Spirit to bring about breakthroughs that go beyond the natural realm, showcasing God's power at work in the world today.

The working of miracles is not a random or whimsical display of power, but a deliberate and intentional act of divine mercy. These miracles are for the benefit of others, fulfilling God's purposes and advancing His kingdom. They are meant to restore what is broken, provide a testimony of God's goodness, and draw people closer to Him. When believers witness or experience miracles, it is not only an opportunity to be amazed but to be reminded that God is actively at work, bringing His kingdom to earth. This powerful gift serves as a testimony to both believers and unbelievers, inviting all into a deeper relationship with the Creator.

Faith plays a crucial role in the working of miracles. Believers are called to step out in bold faith and expectancy, trusting that God can and will act beyond the confines of natural laws. Miracles often challenge human understanding, requiring trust in God's timing and His ability to perform the impossible. In ministry, many testimonies have been shared where miracles have occurred through persistent faith, even when the circumstances appeared impossible. The gift of miracles is not about human ability, but about yielding to God's supernatural power, believing that He can intervene in any situation.

Miracles often work hand-in-hand with other spiritual gifts such as faith and healing. These gifts complement one another and can manifest together in ministry. For instance, healing miracles may go beyond physical restoration and include the miraculous return of sight, the raising of the dead, or the instant healing of severe diseases. When these gifts operate together, they demonstrate the fullness of God's power, working through His people to bring about transformation in the natural world. Believers should remain open to the ways in which these gifts can come together, allowing the Holy Spirit to lead and guide the process.

Humility is essential for those operating in the working of miracles. While God's power flows through believers, it is vital to remember that the miracles are not the result of human effort. The temptation to take credit for these supernatural acts can easily arise, but true servants of God recognize that they are merely vessels through which God's power is made manifest. Believers must remain humble and always give God the glory, acknowledging that it is His power, not their own, that brings about miraculous transformation. This humility allows God to continue to flow through them and empowers them to operate in the gift with purity of heart.

In the process of working miracles, maintaining a close and intimate relationship with the Holy Spirit is vital. The Holy Spirit is the one who empowers believers to operate in this gift, and it is through Him that miracles are made possible. Believers must cultivate sensitivity to the Spirit's leading, listening for His voice and discerning His timing. It is through this deep connection with God that believers can be empowered to step out in faith, trusting that He will work miracles through them. Prayer, worship, and a constant dependence on the Holy Spirit provide the foundation for the miraculous to occur.

Miracles are not confined to the past; they are just as

relevant today as they were in biblical times. God continues to work in powerful ways, performing miracles to demonstrate His love and to reveal His power to a watching world. Believers are encouraged to raise their expectations for supernatural intervention, knowing that God still desires to intervene in miraculous ways. The gift of miracles is available to all believers, and when operated in faith, it can bring profound change in the lives of others, leading them to a deeper understanding of God's love and mercy.

The working of miracles is a gift that can transform lives and impact entire communities. It goes beyond simply meeting needs—it serves as a clear signpost to the glory and power of God, drawing people to Christ. As believers step out in faith, trusting in God's supernatural intervention, they become conduits of His miraculous power. Through these signs and wonders, the world is invited to encounter the reality of God's kingdom on earth. God still desires to work miracles today, and believers are called to be active participants in this divine work, bringing His power to bear in a world desperately in need of His intervention.

In conclusion, the gift of the working of miracles is a powerful and essential aspect of the believer's spiritual toolkit. It requires bold faith, deep intimacy with the Holy Spirit, and a heart of humility and obedience. Through this gift, believers can become agents of transformation, witnessing the supernatural power of God at work in the world around them. When operated in accordance with God's will, the gift of miracles brings about healing, restoration, and breakthrough, advancing His kingdom and drawing people closer to His loving embrace. Through miracles, believers demonstrate the extraordinary nature of God's power and the reality of His kingdom, which continues to break through into the world today.

Reflection Questions:

1. How can you cultivate a greater expectancy and bold faith in your life, trusting God to work miracles in situations that seem impossible?
2. In what ways can you ensure that you remain humble when witnessing or participating in miracles, always giving God the glory for His supernatural work?

Challenge:

THIS WEEK, look for opportunities to step out in faith and pray for a miracle, whether in your own life or on behalf of others. Be open to God's leading, and expect His supernatural intervention. As you do, remember to stay humble and give Him all the glory, acknowledging that it is His power, not yours, that brings about the miracle.

10

The Gift of Prophecy
REVEALING GOD'S HEART

The gift of prophecy is one of the most powerful and transformative gifts given by the Holy Spirit to the body of Christ. It is often misunderstood as being solely for predicting future events, but in reality, prophecy serves to edify, exhort, and comfort the Church. Its primary purpose is to build up believers, encourage them in their faith, and provide direction and hope. When exercised properly, prophecy has the potential to strengthen communities, bring clarity to God's will, and transform individual lives.

Prophecy is not a gift reserved for a select few within the Church. According to Scripture, it is available to all believers, regardless of their position or calling. In 1 Corinthians 14:1, Paul urges Christians to eagerly desire spiritual gifts, especially prophecy. While some individuals may have a stronger prophetic calling, every believer is encouraged to pursue and operate in this gift. By doing so, the body of Christ is strengthened and encouraged, and the believer grows spiritually in the process.

One of the central purposes of prophecy is to build up the body of Christ. It is not intended to create division or confusion. The prophetic ministry should bring comfort, encouragement, and strength to those who receive it, helping them grow in their relationship with God and navigate life's challenges. Prophecy provides revelation and insight into God's heart, illuminating His will for individuals and for the Church as a whole. It should always serve as a tool for spiritual growth, helping believers walk more closely with God.

However, prophecy must always align with Scripture. The Bible is the final authority for believers, and prophecy is not meant to replace or contradict the written Word of God. Instead, it complements the Scriptures, revealing God's heart in ways that align with biblical principles. Every prophetic word must be tested and weighed against the truth of Scripture. Prophecy should be held accountable to church leadership and wise counsel to ensure that it is aligned with God's will and does not lead to confusion or deception.

For those who desire to operate in the gift of prophecy, it is essential to cultivate a deep relationship with God through prayer and worship. The Holy Spirit speaks to those who are sensitive to His leading, and prophetic words should be delivered only when directed by Him. A humble and discerning attitude is necessary when engaging with this gift, recognizing that not every prophetic word is infallible. Prophecy must always be tested by others in the body of Christ, ensuring it is in line with God's purposes and edifies the Church.

Prophets also have a significant role in leadership. They should operate under spiritual authority, submitting their prophetic words to the discernment of church leadership. This helps ensure that the prophetic ministry is used to build up the body of Christ rather than cause division. Prophets should never seek personal gain or pride from their gift; instead, their calling is to serve the Church humbly, revealing God's heart, encouraging others, and helping people align their lives with His will.

The power of prophecy lies in its ability to transform lives and build up the Church. When believers are sensitive to the Holy Spirit and grounded in Scripture, their prophetic words can be a powerful source of encouragement, direction, and strength. Prophecy should always be exercised with the goal of edification, exhortation, and comfort, drawing people closer to God and fostering unity within the Church. A community approach to prophecy, where words are tested and shared for the benefit of all, ensures that the gift is used to strengthen and advance God's kingdom on Earth.

Prophetic ministry is not a personal privilege but a responsibility. Those who are entrusted with the gift of prophecy must approach it with reverence, understanding its purpose to serve others. They should seek to bless the body of Christ rather than gain personal recognition or influence. Prophecy is about revealing God's heart for His people and helping them grow in their relationship with Him. The ultimate goal is to glorify God and advance His kingdom through faithful service to the Church.

In conclusion, the gift of prophecy is a vital tool for spiritual growth and maturity in the body of Christ. It is a powerful way to encourage, strengthen, and comfort others, helping them align their lives with God's will. Every believer is encouraged to seek and operate in this gift, but it must always be exercised with humility, love, and a deep commitment to God's Word. Through prophetic ministry, believers can contribute to the spiritual well-being of the Church, building it up and advancing God's kingdom on Earth.

Reflection Questions:

1. How can you discern the difference between a genuine prophetic word and one that is potentially influenced by personal desires or emotions?
2. In what ways can the gift of prophecy be used to build up the body of Christ while maintaining unity within the Church?

Challenge:

THIS WEEK, commit to cultivating a deeper relationship with the Holy Spirit through prayer and worship. Ask God to give you a heart of humility and discernment to properly steward the gift of prophecy, whether you are receiving or delivering a word, ensuring it aligns with Scripture and serves to encourage and strengthen others.

11

The Gift of Different Kinds of Tongues
A PATH TO SPIRITUAL EDIFICATION

The gift of tongues is a remarkable and distinctive tool in the life of a believer. This gift, though often misunderstood, is one of the most powerful resources for personal growth and spiritual edification. Tongues can take on various forms, ranging from a private prayer language that deepens one's communion with God, to a public expression that brings clarity and encouragement to the Church. This dual purpose of tongues—both for individual edification and corporate ministry—makes it a vital part of a believer's spiritual walk.

The Bible first records the gift of tongues on the Day of Pentecost, where the apostles spoke in languages that were understood by people from diverse regions. These earthly languages were a sign of the Holy Spirit's power at work, enabling people to hear the gospel in their native tongues. This initial outpouring reveals the broad scope of tongues, which encompasses not only known languages but also a supernatural prayer language—one that communicates directly with God. This form of tongues, often unintelligible to the natural mind, allows believers to communicate with the Lord beyond their human limitations, facilitating a deeper intimacy with Him.

In 1 Corinthians 14, the Apostle Paul emphasizes the edifying nature of tongues for personal prayer and spiritual growth. When used privately, speaking in tongues strengthens the spirit of the believer. It bypasses human understanding and enables the worshiper to express praise and supplication to God in a more profound way. As Paul notes, speaking in tongues edifies the individual, helping to build up the inner man and fostering spiritual maturity. Believers are encouraged to cultivate this gift in their private prayer life, using it to grow closer to God and deepen their spiritual walk.

However, tongues is not only for private use—it also serves a significant role in public worship and ministry. When exercised in corporate settings, tongues must be accompanied by interpretation so that the message can be understood by the body of Christ. The purpose of tongues in public worship is not to create confusion, but to bring a word of encouragement, comfort, or exhortation to the congregation. This is why the gift of interpretation is crucial, as it ensures the message of tongues can be communicated effectively for the edification of the Church. In this way, tongues can become a powerful prophetic tool, revealing God's heart and direction for His people.

For tongues to be properly used in the body of Christ, there must be order and discernment. Paul provides clear guidelines for the use of tongues in public worship: no more than two or three individuals should speak in tongues, and they should do so in turn, with interpretation.

This ensures that the congregation is not overwhelmed or confused by an uncontrolled outpouring of tongues. Churches are encouraged to create an atmosphere where the gifts of the Spirit can flow freely but also with careful structure, promoting unity and edification rather than disorder or division.

It is important to maintain balance in the practice of tongues. While tongues is a powerful and beneficial gift, it should never be elevated above other spiritual gifts or used as a source of division within the Church. Misunderstandings surrounding the gift of tongues may lead some to feel hesitant or uncomfortable with it. To avoid this, believers are urged to focus on the overall edification of the body and to ensure that all gifts of the Spirit are operating in harmony. Tongues should be a part of the broader expression of spiritual life, used in moderation and with a focus on building up the Church rather than causing division.

In addition to its role in personal edification and corporate worship, speaking in tongues also provides significant emotional and spiritual benefits. Tongues can be a powerful weapon in spiritual warfare, especially in moments of intercession when the believer is unsure how to pray. The Holy Spirit, praying through the believer, aligns their prayers with God's perfect will, allowing them to engage in warfare with precision and power. Tongues, in this context, becomes a tool for overcoming challenges and aligning with God's purposes in difficult situations.

Believers are encouraged to embrace the gift of tongues with reverence, understanding its profound spiritual impact. When used properly, tongues can lead to deeper intimacy with God, greater spiritual strength, and enhanced ability to intercede for others. However, it is crucial that believers exercise this gift with humility and discernment. Tongues are not a sign of spiritual superiority, but rather a means of engaging with the Holy Spirit in a humble and powerful way, advancing God's kingdom and building up the body of Christ.

In conclusion, the gift of tongues is a dynamic and multifaceted expression of the Holy Spirit's work in a believer's life. Whether used privately for personal edification or publicly to build up the Church, tongues serves to strengthen the believer's spirit and deepen their relationship with God. It is a gift that must be exercised with discernment, order, and humility, always aimed at edifying others and advancing God's kingdom. As believers embrace this gift, they will experience greater intimacy with the Holy Spirit and become more effective in their ministry to the body of Christ.

In conclusion: The gift of tongues is a powerful spiritual tool that can edify individuals and strengthen the Church when used properly. It serves as a personal prayer language that helps believers grow in intimacy with God, and when exercised in public worship, it can bring words of encouragement and guidance to the congregation. By embracing the gift of tongues with humility, balance, and discernment, believers can experience greater spiritual growth and contribute to the health and unity of the body of Christ.

Reflection Questions:

1. How has the gift of tongues personally edified your spiritual life, and in what ways has it deepened your relationship with God?
2. In what ways can you contribute to fostering an atmosphere of order and discernment in your church community when it comes to the use of tongues?

Challenge:

THIS WEEK, make time each day to pray in tongues, seeking deeper intimacy with the Holy Spirit. Reflect on how this practice strengthens your spirit and helps you align your prayers with God's perfect will.

Conclusion
EMBRACING THE GIFTS OF THE SPIRIT FOR SPIRITUAL GROWTH AND KINGDOM IMPACT

Throughout this book, we have explored the diverse and powerful gifts of the Holy Spirit, each uniquely designed to build up the body of Christ, encourage believers, and advance God's kingdom on Earth. From prophecy to tongues, each gift is a tool for spiritual edification, personal growth, and corporate unity. The gifts of the Spirit are not just for a select few but are available to all believers who desire to engage with the Holy Spirit, grow in their relationship with God, and contribute to the life of the Church. It is through these gifts that we are empowered to serve, build one another up, and fulfill the mission God has given us.

As we embrace these gifts, it is essential to remember their primary purpose: to glorify God and edify others. Whether we are operating in the gift of prophecy, healing, or speaking in tongues, our focus should always be on strengthening the body of Christ and helping others grow in their faith. The gifts are not for personal gain or recognition but are meant to serve others and contribute to the common good. When we operate in the gifts with a heart of humility and love, we create an environment where the Holy Spirit can work powerfully through us, transforming lives and advancing God's kingdom.

It is also important to approach the gifts with discernment, balance, and reverence. While the gifts of the Spirit are powerful, they must be exercised according to biblical principles and in alignment with God's Word. This means we should always test prophetic words, seek wise counsel, and use the gifts in an orderly and respectful manner. The gifts should never be used to bring division or confusion, but rather to bring clarity, encouragement, and unity to the Church. By fostering an atmosphere of discernment and order, we ensure that the gifts of the Spirit are used in a way that honors God and builds up His people.

As believers, we are called to cultivate these gifts in our personal lives through prayer, worship, and a deep commitment to spiritual growth. The more we seek the Holy Spirit and surrender to His guidance, the more we will experience the power and beauty of the gifts He has given us. We must not neglect the gifts but instead eagerly desire to operate in them, trusting that the Holy Spirit will equip us for the work He has called us to. When we actively pursue these gifts, we grow in our intimacy with God and become more effective in serving others and fulfilling His purposes on the Earth.

In conclusion, the gifts of the Spirit are an integral part of the Christian life and are essential for spiritual growth, personal transformation, and the advancement of God's kingdom. By embracing these gifts with humility, discernment, and a heart of service, we contribute to the health and unity of the body of Christ. As we continue to walk in the power of the Holy Spirit, let us seek to use our gifts to build up others, glorify God, and fulfill the mission He has entrusted to us. The gifts are not just for today; they are for the building of the Church and the furthering of God's kingdom for generations to come.

About the Author

Tom Cornell is the Senior Leader of SOZO Church in Washington state, founder of Walk in the Light International and SOZO Network. Tom is married to his beautiful wife Katy and lives in the Puget Sound area with her and their three kids. He has been in ministry pastoring and teaching the body of Christ since 2008.

He has a passion to see the body of Christ moving from people with an orphan mindset to that of sonship; equipping the body to do the work of Jesus resulting in seeing the Kingdom of God manifested here on earth.

www.ingramcontent.com/pod-product-compliance
Lightning Source LLC
LaVergne TN
LVHW052038080426
835513LV00018B/2382